WILBRAHAM W9-ANJ-525

Snap books®

Malia and Sasha Obama

by Jennifer M. Besel

CAPSTONE PRESS
a capstone imprint

Snap Books are published by Capstone Press,
151 Good Counsel Drive, P.O. Box 669, Mankato, Minnesota 56002.
www.capstonepub.com

 Books published by Capstone Press are manufactured with paper
containing at least 10 percent post-consumer waste.

Library of Congress Cataloging-in-Publication Data
Besel, Jennifer M.
  Malia and Sasha Obama / by Jennifer M. Besel.
    p. cm.
  Summary: "Describes the lives of Malia and Sasha Obama"—Provided by publisher.
  ISBN 978-1-4296-5000-7 (library binding)
  1. Obama, Malia, 1998—Juvenile literature. 2. Obama, Sasha, 2001—Juvenile literature.
  3. Children of presidents—United States—Biography—Juvenile literature. 4. Obama,
Barack—Family—Juvenile literature. I. Title.
  E909.O25B47 2010
  973.932092'2—dc22
  [B]   2010006578

Editor: Mari Bolte
Designer: Juliette Peters
Media Researcher: Marcie Spence
Production Specialist: Laura Manthe

Photo Credits:
Annie Leibovitz/White House via Getty Images, 21; Aude Guerrucci-Pool/Getty Images, Inc., 15; Callie Shell/MCT/
Landov LLC, 24; Candice C. Cusic/MCT/Landov LLC, 12; Chip Somodeville/Getty Images, Inc., 5; Chuck Kennedy/UPI
Photo/Landov LLC, 6; Frank Polich/Reuters/Landov LLC, 17; Jason Reed/Reuters/Corbis, 9, 11; Jewel Samad/AFP/Getty
Images, Inc., 27; Jim Young/Reuters/Landov LLC, 19; Larry Downing/Reuters/Corbis, cover; Larry Downing/Reuters/
Landov LLC, 23; Lawrence Jackson/White House Handout/CNP/Corbis, 25; Mandel Ngan/AFP/Getty Images, Inc., 14;
Pete Souza/MAI/Landov LLC, 26; Saul Loeb/AFP/Getty Images, Inc., 28; Zbigniew Bzdak/MCT/Landov LLC, 13

Essential content terms are **bold** and are defined at the bottom of the page where they first appear.

Printed in the United States of America in North Mankato, Minnesota.
102010
005971R

Table of Contents

First Daughters

It was January 20, 2009. Malia and Sasha Obama sat together on a stage in front of the U.S. Capitol. They peered out at the sea of people below them.

The day would be one the girls and the world would remember forever. Their father, Barack Obama, was about to be sworn in as president of the United States. More than 1.5 million people stood shoulder-to-shoulder on the streets of Washington, D.C. They had all come to see the man who had won the most historic election of their time.

Even though their family was making history, Malia and Sasha were still regular kids. During the **inauguration** ceremony, they squirmed in their seats during the long speeches. They wiggled to get better views of the performers. Malia snapped pictures of the crowd with her digital camera. Sasha whispered to her mom.

inauguration—the ceremony in which the president is sworn into office

Then the time came for the swearing in ceremony. The family walked to the front of the stage. As the crowd cheered, Sasha jumped onto a stool. Her pink J. Crew jacket and orange scarf blew in the cool breeze. Malia, in a blue coat belted with a satin ribbon, took her place between her sister and mother. The girls watched their father place his hand on Abraham Lincoln's Bible. They listened as he took the oath of office. An African-American family would live in the White House for the first time in U.S. history.

One reporter looked at Sasha's outfit and said, "Orange and pink is the new red, white, and blue."

Time to Party!

That night, it was time to celebrate. The adult Obamas danced the night away at 10 different balls. But Malia and Sasha stayed at the White House for their own party. Accompanied by friends, the girls started the night in their new home's 54-seat theater. They watched *Bolt* and *High School Musical 3*.

After the movies, the White House staff sent the sisters on a scavenger hunt. The girls discovered hidden hideouts and walls that popped open. It was a fun way to learn about their new home.

But that wasn't the night's biggest thrill. The last clue led the girls to the East Room. Inside were the Jonas Brothers! The brothers played three songs. The girls' first night in the White House was filled with perks only stars get. It was a huge change from the life they were used to back in Chicago.

Kids in the White House

Malia and Sasha aren't the first kids to make the White House their home. Just like Sasha, Tad Lincoln was 7 years old when his father, Abraham, became president. Theodore Roosevelt had six children. His kids filled the White House with pets, including a pony, a macaw, dogs, cats, snakes, and even raccoons! In 1961 John F. Kennedy brought his two children to the White House. Caroline was 4 and John Jr. was just a baby. Caroline rode her pony named Macaroni around the White House gardens.

Growing Up an Obama

Although Malia and Sasha are often talked about together, they are very different. They have their own personalities and their own likes and dislikes.

Meet Malia

Malia Ann was born July 4, 1998. Every year on her birthday, the family marches in a Fourth of July parade. Afterward they throw a huge sleepover party for Malia and her friends.

Malia is thoughtful and she considers other people's feelings. She has a positive outlook on life. Barack's nickname for Malia is "Little Miss Articulate" because she has a talent for saying just the right thing.

The president's oldest daughter is also very busy. Malia plays soccer and likes acting in plays. She takes tap dancing and piano lessons too. When she's not bustling from school to activities, Malia loves to crank up her favorite music. Dancing to the Jonas Brothers, Hannah Montana, and Beyoncé is Malia's idea of a great time.

Like her mother, Malia loves wearing the latest trends.

Malia suffers from **asthma** and allergies. Sometimes she has trouble breathing. She has medicine that helps her, and she doesn't let asthma slow her down. When she needs a little comfort, she still hugs her favorite stuffed animal, Tiger. Malia and Tiger have been a pair since Malia was 3 years old.

Spunky Sasha

Sasha was born June 10, 2001. Sasha is actually a nickname. Her real name is Natasha, but she is hardly ever called that. Her presidential papa calls her his "precious pea." Sasha is a spunky girl, known for her sense of humor and wide smiles. She prefers high fives to handshakes. She's been seen giving Vice President Joe Biden and former Vice President Dick Cheney slaps on the hand!

Sasha loves to be in the spotlight. Like her sister, Sasha is busy. She does gymnastics and tap dances. She also takes piano lessons. Her parents make sure she has plenty of time for playdates with friends.

When Sasha was just 3 months old, she developed meningitis. This infection makes the membranes around the brain and spinal cord swell. If it's not treated in time, meningitis can be deadly. Under the care of doctors and nurses, Sasha recovered.

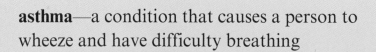

asthma—a condition that causes a person to wheeze and have difficulty breathing

Sasha often smiles and waves to reporters.

Powerful Parents

To the world, Barack and Michelle Obama are superstars. But to Sasha and Malia, they're just Mom and Dad.

Barack was born in Hawaii in 1961. Barack worked as a community organizer, helping improve life for people in poor neighborhoods. He went to Harvard and became a lawyer.

His desire to help people led him to run for public office. Barack served eight years in the Illinois State **Senate**. In 2004 he was elected to the U.S. Senate. Barack moved to Washington, D.C., while Michelle, Malia, and Sasha stayed in Chicago. The distance was hard on the family. But Barack hoped to be an example to his daughters. He wanted them to learn to help people too.

Malia and Sasha have a great role model in their father.

Senate—one of the two houses of some governments that makes laws; the U.S. government and states have senates

Malia (3) and Sasha (6) posed with their mom at their home in Chicago.

Malia and Sasha also look up to their mother. Michelle Robinson was born in 1964 in Chicago. She earned a law degree from Harvard. She became a powerful leader in Chicago, developing community service programs. But even though she had a very busy schedule, Michelle always made sure that her children came first.

" ... I come here as a mom, as a mom whose girls are the heart of my heart and the center of my world."
—Michelle Obama in her speech at the 2008 Democratic National Convention.

Sasha helped her father fill backpacks for children of members of the U.S. military.

Helping People

Before moving into the White House, Malia and Sasha lived on the South Side of Chicago. The Obama family had a big, gated home worth $1.65 million. But the South Side is not known for its million-dollar homes. Instead, many poor people live there. Malia and Sasha saw how hard life could be for some people in their community. And they learned the importance of helping others from their mom and dad.

Family Time

Staying close as a family is also very important to the Obamas. But with a dad who worked in Washington, D.C., staying close was tough. While serving in the U.S. Senate, Barack's days were filled with meetings. Malia and Sasha often only talked to their dad on the phone each night. So the girls relied on their mother. One of the sisters' favorite things to do was climb in bed with their mom in the morning. They spent time just having girl talk.

When dad was home, the Obamas made the most of their time together. Malia and her dad read all the Harry Potter books together. He listened to Sasha practice on the piano. The family played games like Uno and went to the zoo.

Malia helped President Obama serve meals in honor of Martin Luther King Jr. Day in Washington, D.C.

On the Campaign Trail

In 2007 Barack and Michelle made a big decision. Barack would run for president of the United States. They knew the decision wouldn't just affect them. It would change their daughters' lives too.

The Obama family found themselves in the spotlight. Reporters followed their every move. Pictures of the girls eating ice cream, trick-or-treating, and going to school were everywhere. The family did photo shoots and interviews.

Even though there was a lot going on, Michelle did her best to keep life normal at home. She would catch a flight to an event in the morning. Then she would return home in time to tuck the girls into bed. Sasha and Malia still had to follow household rules. They had to be in bed by 8:30 p.m., and they could only watch one hour of TV a day. They also had to make their beds and clean their rooms.

Sasha and Malia were with their parents when Barack announced that he would run for president.

Keeping it Real

While their parents **campaigned** across the country, Malia and Sasha went to school. The sisters went to a private school called the University of Chicago Laboratory Schools. They were expected to do their very best. In fact, Barack and Michelle went to the girls' parent-teacher conferences the day after the presidential election.

campaign—to try to gain support from people in order to win an election

No matter how hard she tried, Michelle couldn't be in two places at once. Sometimes she just couldn't get home. During those times, Malia and Sasha's grandmother, Marian Robinson, took care of the girls. She helped with homework, took Sasha and Malia to the dentist, and did other everyday things. The girls are very close to their grandmother, who still cares for her grandchildren in the White House.

When the girls didn't have school, they attended a day camp or traveled with their parents. While their mom gave speeches, they stayed in hotels and swam in the pools. When their dad was gaining support at a picnic, the girls took their shoes off and practiced hula hooping. The cameras were always on them. But Malia and Sasha were calm. They didn't let the attention bother them. They just tried to have fun.

"Are you going to try to be president? Shouldn't you try to be vice president first?"
—Malia, talking to her father about his campaign for president.

Sasha and Malia wore cream and white J. Crew jackets at a celebration at the Lincoln Memorial.

Looking Like an Obama

Malia and Sasha have become the "it girls" when it comes to style. Reporters snap pictures of them wherever they go. Girls around the world copy what the first daughters wear. When people saw Sasha's orange and pink outfit at the inauguration, they demanded to know where it was from. The girls' fun, yet reasonably priced, wardrobe has people hitting store shelves to dress like the famous first sisters.

The first family's hair gets attention too. In summer 2009, Malia went on vacation sporting trendy twists in her hair. Young African-American girls flocked to the salon to get the same look. When she decided to let her hair fall naturally, Malia didn't realize she was setting a trend.

A Big Move

On January 20, 2009, Barack was sworn in as president of the United States. And the girls moved to a new house. It wasn't just any house though. It was the White House!

The president and his family moved into the second and third floors of the White House. The first family could decorate it any way they wanted. Although they were offered a redecorating allowance, the family used their own money. They set a budget of $100,000 to redo their living area. To keep costs down, they decorated their new digs with things from Target, Pottery Barn, and Crate and Barrel. The girls picked out the colors of their rooms. They also brought their Jonas Brothers posters from home!

The Obama family had an official portrait taken in the White House's Green Room.

Being the Presidential Family

For several years, the Obama family had been split between Chicago and Washington, D.C. Living in the White House, the girls see their dad every day. At night, the family eats supper together. During supper, they play a game called "roses and thorns." Each person tells the rosy part of their day and the thorny part. Just having time together has made the family closer.

What a House!

It's a good thing Sasha and Malia have years to explore their new home. The house has 132 rooms and 35 bathrooms. For fun, there's a swimming pool, tennis court, and bowling lane. And don't forget about the theater. The White House has a deal set up with Hollywood. If Sasha or Malia want to see a movie that isn't out yet, they just have to ask. The Motion Picture Association will deliver it to them for free.

Hungry? The White House has five full-time chefs who can make the sisters anything they want. They often ask for their favorite foods—fried chicken and macaroni and cheese. What an amazing place to live!

The family greets guests from the Truman Balcony of the White House. From left are Barack, Sasha, Michelle, Marian Robinson, and Malia.

But just like in Chicago, the girls are expected to do chores. Michelle told the White House staff not to pick up after Malia and Sasha. The girls have to clean their rooms and make their beds. They also have to help clear the dishes after supper. If they do their chores, they earn a $1 a week allowance.

Barack and Michelle saw their daughters off on their first day at Sidwell Friends.

A New School

Being the president's daughters doesn't get you out of school or homework. Malia and Sasha changed schools when they moved to Washington, D.C. They now go to a private school called Sidwell Friends. The school has taught presidential children since Theodore Roosevelt's children went there.

Malia goes to the middle school campus in Washington, D.C. Sasha's elementary school is a few miles away in Bethesda, Maryland. Malia and Sasha had a headstart on making friends at their new school. Joe Biden's grandchildren also go to Sidwell Friends. Sasha and Malia had friends at their new school before they even started! The president has also been spotted dropping the girls off at school (accompanied by Secret Service agents, of course!)

A New Family Member

During Barack's campaign for president, Malia and Sasha were promised a special present. After the election, they would get a puppy. Malia spent hours researching dogs. People shouted ideas to the girls wherever they went. All over the country, people weighed in on what dog the Obamas should get.

The family finally settled on a black-and-white Portuguese water dog they call Bo. Bo fits right into their family. And he's perfect for Malia—his fur doesn't upset her allergies. Everyone takes turns caring for the dog. Malia and Sasha scoop poop from the White House lawn. The president walks Bo at night.

Bo's likeness has been captured as a stuffed toy, a watch face, and even a comic book hero!

America's Princesses

Living in the White House has changed the way the Obama family lives. The girls can't go to the playground whenever they want anymore. So their parents bought a brand new play set, which was built right outside the Oval Office. The set, which cost the family $3,500, has a slide, fort, climbing wall, and swings. Malia and Sasha like to have their friends from school over to play on the play set.

The play set was a surprise for Malia and Sasha. It was set up while the girls were in school.

The family traveled to Oahu, Hawaii, in December 2009.

Then there's the traveling. During their first summer vacation as presidential daughters, Malia and Sasha traveled the world. The family started in Paris, visiting the Eiffel Tower and eating lunch with the French president. In England, they got a tour of Buckingham Palace from Queen Elizabeth II and visited the Harry Potter movie set. In Italy, they learned to make gelato, an Italian dessert. They met the pope. In December 2009, the family traveled to Hawaii, where they enjoyed shaved ice and watched the movie *Avatar*.

Always Watched

Being famous has its downsides too. **Paparazzi** follow the family wherever they go, taking pictures and asking questions.

Being part of the presidential family is also a bit dangerous. There are people who may try to harm the president or his family. Malia and Sasha are followed everywhere by Secret Service agents. These highly trained bodyguards protect the sisters from any harm.

Everyone in the family has a code name. The names all start with the same letter. Barack is Renegade and Michelle is Renaissance. Malia is known as Radiance and Sasha is called Rosebud.

"First African-American president. Better be good."
—Malia, talking to her father while visiting the Lincoln Memorial.

paparazzi—aggressive photographers who take pictures of celebrities for sale to magazines or newspapers

Making History

Malia and Sasha will forever be part of American history. In the past, presidential children have been left out of **media** coverage. But Sasha and Malia have become mega-stars. People flock to Web sites about them. A toy company made Sasha and Malia dolls. Fans even watch the first daughters for clothing and hairstyle trends.

No one knows what the future holds for Malia and Sasha Obama. These fun-loving kids have a lot of time before they have to decide. For right now, they're just having fun being kids—who happen to be the nation's first daughters.

media—forms of communication that send out messages to large groups of people, like TV, radio, and newspapers

Glossary

asthma (AZ-muh)—a condition that causes a person to wheeze and have difficulty breathing

campaign (kam-PAYN)—to try to gain support from people in order to win an election

inauguration (i-NAW-gyur-ray-shun)—the ceremony in which the president of a country is sworn into office

media (MEE-dee-uh)—TV, radio, newspapers, and other communication forms that send out messages to large groups of people

meningitis (men-in-JYE-tis)—a disease that causes the membranes around the brain and spinal cord to swell

paparazzi (pah-puh-RAHT-see)—aggressive photographers who take pictures of celebrities for sale to magazines or newspapers

Senate (SEN–it)—one of the two houses of some governments that makes laws; the U.S. government and states have senates

Read More

Snyder, Gail. *Malia.* The Obamas: First Family of Hope. Broomall, Penn.: Mason Crest, 2009.

Snyder, Gail. *Sasha. The Obamas:* First Family of Hope. Broomall, Penn.: Mason Crest, 2009.

Zumbusch, Amelie von. *First Family: The Obamas in the White House.* Making History: The Obamas. New York: PowerKids Press, 2010.

Internet Sites

FactHound offers a safe, fun way to find Internet sites related to this book. All of the sites on FactHound have been researched by our staff.

Here's all you do:

Visit *www.facthound.com*

FactHound will fetch the best sites for you!

Index